Ghazals for Foley

— edited by —

Yago S. Cura

Ghazals for Foley

— A Collection of Ghazals and Ghazal-Like Poetry —

Collected to Honor JAMES W. FOLEY, American Combat Journalist.

featuring:

Compound Memorandum

by

JAMES FOLEY
{ a short story originally published by HINCHAS Press }

HINCHASPress
Los Angeles

© Copyright Yago Cura, 2022. All rights reserved.
No part of this book may be reproduced in any manner whatsoever without written permission from the publisher, except in the case of brief quotations in critical reportage and reviews.

Illustration by Carlos Folgar.
Design by Autumn Anglin.

Printed in the United States
By IngramSpark, Lightning Source LLC
1246 Heil Quaker Blvd, La Vergne, TN 37086

Names: Cura, Yago, 1975 - editor
Title: Ghazals for Foley / Yago Cura
Description: Los Angeles, CA : Hinchas de Poesia Press (HINCHAS Press), [2022]
ISBN# 978-0-9845398-5-7 (Print edition)
ISBN# 978-1-954640-96-2 (Ebook edition)
Subjects: Poetry

HINCHAS Press (Hinchas de Poesía Press) is a Los Angeles-based micropress that publishes zines, poetry, poetry in translation, and library science non-fiction. In line with the rabid fanaticism that defines fútbol (soccer) fans in Latin America, HINCHAS channels the best aspects of that energy and gives a voice to non-traditional and marginalized communities, supports social justice initiatives, and advocates for bilingual literacy endeavors, especially along portions of the Américas that are monolingual.

Learn more about HINCHAS Press (hinchaspress.com), our defunct online literary journal, Hinchas de Poesía (www.hinchasdepoesia.com), and the eternal debt of gratitude we owe to James Wright Foley (1973 – 2014), American combat journalist that had the moral courage to report on the atrocities being committed against the Syrian people by the Assad regime.
Please direct all inquiries to:

Yago Cura, HINCHAS Press
yagoscura@gmail.com

Also available from HINCHAS PRESS: *Bringer of Culture* – Jim Heavily | *Inspiring Library Stories* – Oleg Kagan | *Librarians with Spines* – Max Macias and Yago S. Cura, eds. | *Librarians with Spines Vol. II* – Max Macias and Yago S. Cura, eds. | *Odas a Futbolistas* – Yago S. Cura & Abel M. Folgar | *X LA Poets* – Linda Ravenswood, ed. | *Tlacuilx: Tongues in Quarantine*, poetry by Project 1521 | *Renault 30* – Abel M. Folgar

Ghazals for Foley was completely funded by a successful Kickstarter campaign that was launched on March 3, 2015. The only reason this book is in your hand right now is because of donations made to that campaign.
HINCHAS Press would like to thank all the donors that gave to that campaign for making this volume possible, and all the contributors who allowed us to publish their ghazals and raise money for the James W. Foley Legacy Fund.

HINCHASPress is the imprint of the digital codex of contemporary Pan-American writing, Hinchas de Poesía (www.hinchasdepoesia.com). As such, it publishes the fiction, poetry, and prose of authors from las Américas; therefore, if you are from América, and write poetry, fiction, or criticism on elements of the transcontinental diaspora of América, then we invite you to submit your work. In terms of taste and content, Hinchas de Poesía believes the content to be the medium. To that end, we publish innovative, experimental work of a devastating caliber, regardless of format or dialect. Please send us work you are unsure about, using language that belies the contours of a nameless gloss.
FoleyBook_

Contents

Introduction | *Yago S. Cura*

G for F for E | *Adolfo Guzman-Lopez*

Ghazal for James Wright Foley | *Daniel Johnson*

Breath Ghazal | *D.N. Pace*

J. Mascis at the 13th Floor | *Connoly Ryan*

Nada Messiah Ghazal | *Matt Basiliere*

part three | *Ruben Cruz*

Ghazal with Owls | *Susie Meserve*

Ghazal for Jim | *Brian Jordan*

Ghazal for Hamza-Foley | *Yago S. Cura*

Ghost Tongue | *Kevin Goodan*

The Granite State | *Sejal Shah*

Ghazal | *Chris Van Dyke*

A Ghazal for Jim Foley | *C.S. Carrier*

Ghazal of Witness | *Daniel Mahoney*

Bad Sufi Feeling | *Claire Morgana Gillis*

GHAZAL [JIM] | *Ethan Paquin*

The Blue Sea Seemed Further Than It Was | *Yaddyra Peralta*

Ghazal for a Tall Boy From New Hampshire | *Martín Espada*

Rt. 25, Indiana | *Ben Balthaser*

Poem 52: for Jim Foley | *Andew Varnon*

Illocution & Colors | *Rachelle Linda Escamilla*

Christmas Poem for Jim Foley | *Mike Dockins*

Ghazal | *Shauna Seliy*

In the Absence of Sparrows* | *Daniel Johnson*

Compound Memorandum | *James Foley*

Introduction

> — "Before you make another speech, make sure your bike can reach"
> Tanya Stephens, "Ninja Bike"

> —"For a free-verse ghazal is a contradiction in terms. As perhaps a free-verse sonnet, arguably, is not?
> Agha Shahid Ali

You have in your hands a book of ghazals and ghazal-like poetry collected by the friends of James Wright Foley; accordingly, it is rife with the writing of the students of Writing Jim studied with at the Poets and Writers graduate program, and undergraduate Writing Program at ZooMass-Amherst. In March of 2015, through individual, private donations to Kickstarter (www.kickstarter.com), we were able to collect almost $1,300.00 to publish a book of ghazals written to, about, or for Jim.

The idea to publish a book of ghazals for Jim came to us after having read an October 25, 2014 NY Times article, "The Horror Before the Beheadings." The article discusses Jim's conversion to Islam while he was being held in Syria. Naturally, the article begs the question of whether "any conversion under such duress [is] a legitimate one"? I like to think the article also addresses how maybe Jim's biggest act of defiance was synchronizing his spirituality with that of his captors, that way they (and Jim) would all know that when they tortured Jim they were torturing a convert and neophyte—not just some immoral, opulent Westerner. Jim was one of the best guys, used by some of the worst people, to achieve some sort of low-brow, reactionary end.

Using the ghazal's form to "speak" with Jim made sense to us, I guess, because of how the repetition crescendos, and because the form has addressed separation, mourning, and loss for centuries. Given his recent conversion, maybe, we are hoping to "talk" to Jim using a form he might more easily authenticate? Maybe, we chose to write to him in a dialect that forces us to traipse in clunky, couplet boots because what we've come to say is painful and devastating, so much so that to say it out loud with our very own lips seems inexorable? We kept the editorial bar low, greedily accepting as many submissions as we could. Some of these poems are ghazals and some, decidedly, are not. But, these poems are a collection of mourning stones, a surtido of cairns indexed for gross circulation— poetry from the sky, from el mero ether. Besides, why shouldn't we write poems to Jim in a form that according to the Academy of American Poets was "often sung by Iranian, Indian, and Pakistani musicians" ("Ghazals," par. 2).You have in your hands a rock Paul Pierce might have shot to Bird before Bird shoved it down the gullet of an orange overtime.

The year before Jim and I were set to start at ZooMass, a poetry professor there, Agha Shahid Ali, assembled a book of ghazals, Ravishing DisUnities: Real Ghazals in English (Wesleyan Press, 2000) that contains more than one hundred "ravishing" ghazals, and establishes linguistic and historical criteria poets can utilize to contradict petty claims championed by many American poets about the sonnet being our oldest poetic form. Rumi and Hafiz, whom garnered the ghazal "prominence in the thirteenth-and fourteenth-century" ("Ghazals," par. 2) are its great grandfathers, but Goethe, that most German of German writers, actually stands as the ghazal's Western representative and unofficial ambassador, having popularized the form in West-östlicher Divan (1819), a Romantic staple.

You hold in your hands Memorex of a life led in service to the destitute and the jagged, those worn down by poverty's thresher. This book is no codex of exemplars for a "minimum of five couplets—and typically no more than fifteen" ("Ghazals," par.1). However, we all know how to write a Ghazal, right? According to the Academy of American Poets, "The first couplet introduces a scheme, made up of a rhyme followed by a refrain. Subsequent couplets pick up the same scheme in the second line only, repeating the refrain and rhyming the second line with both lines of the first stanza." ("Ghazals," par. 1). Again, though, in his introduction to DisUnities, Ali's schematics concerning the self-replicating Skynet of the ghazal prove leagues more crystalline.

> The opening couple (called matla) sets up the scheme (of rhyme called qafia; and refrain-called radif) by having it occur in both lines—the rhyme IMMEDIATELY preceding the refrain—and then this scheme occurs only in the second line of each succeeding couplet (3).

Most of the contributors to this collection were very close friends of James Foley, but many of the contributors had never met the young combat journalist, educator, and philanthropist. In the way spectacles decimate the known, all of the contributors are innocent bystanders unequivocally grieved by the senseless, insidious, murder of Jim. All contributors to Ghazals for Foley offer their outpouring in writing, and seek to respect the permutations of ideas, friends, and spiritualities Jim was known to traffic in.

All the contributors to this project have donated their pieces para la causa, and any proceeds from the first printing of Ghazals for Foley are being donated by Hinchas Press (www.hinchasdepoesia.com) to the James W. Foley Legacy Foundation.

Hinchas will print and provide an ISBN (International Standard Book Number) and will distribute copies first to donors whom helped us raise $1,300.00 on Kickstarter, and then to vendors, distributors, and interested libraries from Los Angeles to points east. You hold in your hands a gaggle of Ghazals, written by brothers and colleagues, adherents and laggards, bunglers, paladins—anything but nihilists.

In your hands, that artifact: a terrestrial attempt to assure Jim we are still writing, still pushing, still turning up to workshops with pages, still uttering uncomfortable truths about our roles in the worlds we inhabit, and our complicity in worlds we choose to ignore. In your hands: a flare gun, dirty brass ensemble, something immense to correct with a red pen—a corral of tweaks. You hold something many of us have wanted improvised for a while now, so hold fast.

— *Yago S. Cura*

G for F for E
Adolfo Guzman-Lopez

Because we will not, the seer must stare, taste, hurt, squint, crouch.
Desert light burns through cartridge-loading and kids crutch-walking.

These big city dance halls sweat with laughter, brotherhood-sisterhood.
Come to escape the black-hooded hands squeezing a country, its eyes.

The dancing life and the asking life hold hands on the couplet stage.
Five Levant stars are blown Altamira-like onto a rising white curtain.

The face at the table in front of me is human; I love it like yours.
Faces waltz, wonder as the needle backtracks on the last groove.

See and feel the scattered pieces of my prisoner of war map.
I will crash land on your skin, roll up the scroll, start from end.

Ghazal for James Wright Foley

Daniel Johnson

> —"The idea of walking ahead on my own through the desert
> as if compelled by a magnet is insane."
> **James Foley** in his Syria journal

Kinetic friend, you moved like light in a mirrored room. Come home.
Raqqa. Damascus. Aleppo. Homs. You rarely took a room. Come home.

We'll read Borges aloud–burn windfall in the pit–spark a joint.
You'd leave a parting gift, a rebel scarf or Turkish cartoon. Come home.

You crashed your Civic reading Chomsky in Chicago traffic.
Who now will shatter the day into such bright ruins? Come home.

I killed a bat in Olanna's room, its body the size of a grape.
I laid it in the trash on eggshells like broken stones. Come home.

Roethke in his journals wrote— The cage is open. You may go.
If sunlight bleeds under your cell door, Jim, never the moon. Come home.

Breath Ghazal
D.N. Pace

Wind blows through the trees as a bird flies over,
whirring in the nether that will be-a breath.

Life stumbles and tumbles as we crash, exist-
nevermore pondering, just awaiting-breath.

Stand amid shadows of broken-hearted pain
with Cheshire grin, joyous peace, love, and breath.

Embrace all the world; show compassion and love-
lunge toward adventure like a colt's first breath.

Wishes and hopes linger through embattled days.
None know, understand, foresee: Just...take...deep...breaths.

Left to wonder of a life fully lived, and yet
uncertain of what comes, in spite of deep breaths.

Pain and joy come into themselves as thoughts flood
bewildered minds like a sprinter gasps for breaths.

Laughter permeates midnight hours as light
shatters the alcoves of anxious minds with breath.

J. Mascis at the 13th Floor

Connoly Ryan

There are no words, but if there were:
long-lasting blasts of glassblowing elasticity
stretching the future and contesting space itself.
It felt like my brain and groin has just received free gravity
lessons for the next three hundred years.
Thrusts of rogue voltage and illogical wattage took aim.
A pulverization of absolutes ensued.

Earlier in the day I had skipped a memorial
for a friend because sometimes the world is unbearable
and I didn't want to be in a room surrounded
by people who know it.: a roomful of some
who had known and some who loved
a friend who had been beheaded, Jim Foley.
Instead I biked to a tiny local venue
and saw a man play guitar.
I have never been in a room
with someone who knew more exactly
what he was doing than he did last night.
He unloaded, in detonative increments,
a murder of scarecrows and welded a guild
of levitating Tin-Men. He did to music what both Dylans
did to the dictionary: clobbered it, seduced it, released it
and smoked it with ceremonial respect. The little bar room
only took a few seconds to become a cathedral
of uncouth catharsis, a mosque of aches and strokes,
a synagogue gurgling in a melting bog, a childhood
in the woods, a graveyard in reverse.

Latticework melodies driving
an almost Mr Bill-like falsetto, mesmerizing
and plasmatic, generating that skipping-stones-on-a-pond
with-your-cool-uncle type of reassurance and calm..
And then he went and pushed the distortion pedal
and summoned Kubrick, Hendrix, Man Ray, You Name It
and a long profusion of twittering machines and clockwork
derangements saner and serener than anything yet saturated
in spastic lunacy all the same.

As if peyote and bagpipes got high and fucked the rain.
As if fatigue and lethargy disappeared and were replaced
by exultancy and genius; his acoustic guitar, a druid prayer
for all the dead legends who know not their own death,
cradled in his calculated maniacal arms like a pagan bride.

One is not supposed to be able
to do what he was doing last night,
to sound what he was sounding;
but, he was doing it and sounding it as though
there was nothing ever else
he was supposed to have been doing.
And, we, his audience, awed and flayed, were also
exactly in the spot our whole lives had directed us toward
in that dark room, stunned and planted, stone free
and rising—each strange note a death-mask kiss,
every nerve and sense laid bare and filled
with answered longing and a haunted ringing.

Like all masters of narrative, he began in the middle
of a traumatized frenzy, Zeus having a seizure, a shark
attacking a lifeguard whose wife has left him anyway;
putting on a clinic of melancholy and resolution, providing
and removing the edge from the edge and, against all
sentiment and logic, UN-beheading my friend Jim Foley,
(in my mind at least,) so that I could close my eyes and see
Jim smiling his intractable smile, intact and relaxed,
poised at the other end of this intimate room
taking everything in as though it really were everything.
When I opened my eyes to the unceasing mercy of Mascis's
blossom-blooded, mist-fisted dirge and my friend Jim
was not there, was not there...;

but where he was and is the music is reaching him yet,
is fetching him, is making him return,
because the music, though perilous and imperiled,
is peaceful and secure at its core and only through
its vigilant language
does endless torture
ever meet its timely end.

Nada Messiah Ghazal
Matt Basiliere

There are so many people who claim so much more for themselves than their taut
Skin and wide smiles. And I've seen how they've grown.

I've seen them burn through the world like angels, clear paths before them.
And when those paths didn't deliver them home, I've seen how they've grown.

I've seen the metrics, the images—shorn scalp; an orange qamis; a torso on a Martian landscape—Hold,
flicker then still. And watching those images I've seen how they've grown

Into the stupidest, most predictable fucking storylines ever. Sanctified before one word was spoken.
But in darkness, when storylines tangle in tears and mute dreams, I've seen how they've grown

Back into one body—laughing, yo—as water cools your throat and over your taut skin ripple hosts,
Not of angels, Jim, but grass leaves—fresh, untrammeled. In sunshine I've seen how they've grown.

Part Three
Ruben Cruz

in between the living room sessions of satanic verses, to the freestyles on

the red/brown/green/orange/blue line well past midnight— if you care to

search hard enough, the stories are out there

from every pained look, captured in every gasping breath, between the

pillars of concrete fortresses lining the mean Chicago streets—

if you care to search hard enough, the stories are there

blaring from the peoples orchestra through the enchanting rhythms

of the deep pounding congas and the clean precision of the rapid-fire cajons—

if you care to search hard enough the stories are in there

on stage before an inviting crowd, w/ wild fury of heart, a mind full of

Cesar's dank buds & poetry at the lips,

if you care to search hard enough the stories are out there

smoking a spliff on diece-ocho, w/ Tata outside in the dead of winter,

with only the sound of the freezing winds to keep us company

if you care to search hard enough the stories are out there

in the abandoned empty churches, where the last of the hopeful seek

refuge from the powers that be

if you care to search hard enough the stories are still there from the cracked-out dungeons of the district capitols, to the wretched

filth-covered lives of the Main Streeters

if you care to search hard enough the stories are there

in between the I.E.D.S, & in the small-town raids, where military aid is

but a bullet or casket

if you care to search hard enough the stories are there

in the bombed-out bunkers & villas, suites and palaces of former U.S.

backed dictators

if you care to search hard enough the stories are there

around the bonfire of confiscated hashish burning in the Afghani night

if you care to search hard enough the stories are out there

from the Colorado, to the Mississippi, the Euphrates, to the River Jordan

in these sacred waters of lifeif you care to search hard enough the stories

are there

inside that small junior high classroom deep in the ghetto centrally

located in the heart of the desert you cared to search hard enough, for

the stories were there.

Ghazal with Owls
Susie Meserve

All lost time runs by in your dreams
Are you still alive in your dreams?

Owls screeched the night you were blasphemed
Barred, barn, great horned, like a dream.

First my nightmare: scared, you keened—
Then the raptors pried me from my dreams.

No form of prayer made you strigine
Your stories still survive in my dreams.

I'll not ask of the paper in reams
Nightbird, did you cry in your dreams?

Nor of your night-times, horrific scene
Profane, I thought to tithe for your dreams.

Jannah keep you, enchanted and lean
Your body wing-lithe, shy as a dream.

Sing me Susie, one word clean
Then you, Jim, fly by in my dreams.

Ghazal for Jim

Brian Jordan

Lost in Wideman's Great Time, driving through the late summer air
in no hurry, nightflies getting closer

Talking about what we're going to do—those mountains in the
distance— sunrise getting closer.

So solid, whatever it was. I always knew I was safe with you.
Your close reads, your solid screens
Your hand on my arm pulling me out of that Holyoke bar, trouble (and lies)
getting closer.

Floating down the hill toward the chimes, toward mass at dusk deep
into the silent retreat
Looking over across all those seekers with your loving, laughing eyes—
for a moment I get closer.

Linda—"Timmy, stop crying."—in the O'Brien story, and Patricia sweeping,
sweeping in yours
And that little girl on the table in Aleppo they pleaded with you to show,
as you keep moving in closer and closer.

So easy to imagine it different, you covering Latin America now, flying out to
San Salvador or somewhere tonight
I'll meet you at Logan for a beer and tell you everything I remember, aware
of the clock, your flight time getting closer.

Ghazal for Hamza-Foley

Yago S. Cura

> —"Mr. [James] Foley converted to Islam soon after his capture and adopted the name Abu Hamza"
> *Oct. 25, 2014 N.Y. Times article.*

Hard for me to believe Jimbo didn't convert under duress.
Although, I have always known him spiritually curious.

Easier to believe he proved syrup at fangs of alien vampires
intent on making him pay, leaving us lot spiritually curious.

Jimbo adopts name Abu Hamza because Hamza's famous
for riding into Battle of Badir with an ostrich feather in his turban.
(how spiritually curious of him, no doubt!).

Hamza was a late convert to Islam; Jimbo came to journalism a
seasoned teacher.
Both proved paladin interlopers, distinguished ball-busters of spirit:
eminently curious.

También, the manner in which both are cut down early in life, apenitas
after egress of civilians on H.D.M.I. proves too easy for Western media,
of little spiritual curiosity.

Tell me Abu, how could you have known that an Abyssinian slave would
gamble on their manumission by chucking a javelin into the abdomen of an
O.G.-General?
You'd have to be spiritually curious, que no?

How does one roam into a 'sitch so egregiously far from Lake Winnipesaukee?
How does one prevent their liver from turning into jewelry of spiritual curiosities?

Jimbo picks Moe's right-hand man (I'm talking about Hamza here) because Jimbo knows Gabriel only shows himself to deniers of emerald escalators, not the spiritually curious.

Tell me Abu, why should I forgive the rabid—the rabbled, wracked with graphic cabals?
Estos matadores en balaclavas tyranny the Just, pimp the Innocent, and claim spiritual curiousity.

Torture ain't stop Jimbo programming though: specialist lectures, tournaments of Risk, faux wrestling matches between captives, inter-captive wrestling matches. For what? Morale, and to not lose spirit and curiosity.

Abu is kindness performed with militance; Jimbo is witness subsumed with service.
Together they shatter cisterns, premonition sprouts, solace the voiceless, curiously.

Ghost Tongue

Kevin Goodan

We begin with a voice, not a mute throat—
Stars/letters, language/light. God's house is no mute throat.

I breathe forests into flame to seduce the devil—
I'll bind you. I'll cut the heat from your mute throat.

Beloved demon (damn you), help me unstring the snare
Of ruby pearls from around your mute throat.

We pray, every martyr, for you, for rain, not dust
And we are granted the sun in our mute throats.

O huntress, my caged gazelle, if I kiss your thighs
Will you scream the words of my mute throat?

Shadow, I beseech you, lift up these arms.
Wound in my side? See the fletching of my mute throat?

Desert air is made of blood. Dawn above the minarets
Is witness to small birds rising from your mute throat.

Speak, now. I was named out of fear. James, were you?
I, who refused to portray death with such a mute throat.

The Granite State

Sejal Shah

I see you, Jim, at seventeen, on a VHS tape transferred to digital, and then my memory.
A New Hampshire quiz show, projected on your 41st birthday dinner—
also your memorial.

The drive back to Rochester, New York from your Rochester is now autumnal memory.
Nine hours of traffic on my birthday—the day after your birthday, also falls into memory.

We are (were) both Libras. Scales, balanced? Not me. No one disliked you in my memory.
Each state has a motto—each state a rock, a bird, a flower, a capitol, an archive: memory.

Live Free or Die is the easiest (if from New England or a writer), to commit to memory.
What is mine? The Empire State is not an image, nor anything to attach to memory.

I knew you best in 2000, before I lost my heart, before the towers' museum and memorial.
Empire is a building once tallest, then overtaken by towers, falling figures, and now memory.

You were the tallest of Jim, Will, Brian, Chris, Yago—though Dan was taller — one memory.
Another is dancing with you, salsa—our knees knocking into one another, my silly memory.

Wikipedia tells me the state rock of New York is garnet—dark red— Adirondack memory.
I want to not know the state rock of New Hampshire. I do. I now carry this memory.

I unearth your workshop comments from a box in my parents' basement, doubting memory.
You wrote two pages of comments, your name, then one last run-on: now-cherished memory.

I like the pathos you lay out there, your writing is risky, barbs underneath a fleecy texture. This memory.
I am pleased you call my writing risky. I will replace all other memories with this memory.

I see you, even younger, on Granite State Challenge. You guessed wrong, now tender memory.
The celebration, candles lit & held, skits, conjuring you, witness!—repository of your memory.

My fiancé and I attended—in one day—your birthday party—your mass—your memorial.
It was your wedding as well: our gathering your reception. I did marry.
I carry your memory.

Ghazal

Chris Van Dyke

I have been asked to write a poem in an ancient style that I have never seen
in memory of a man I never knew, who died in a land I have never seen.

It is a strangely somber task to write of a stranger's death, a human life
forced into abstraction, reduced to the mere concept of mourning, a face never seen,

except in news articles and obituaries, on FaceBook feeds and pages
voicing outrage at his death, nothing tangible, nothing ever heard, ever seen.

It is a strange and somber task to write of a stranger's death, oddly
self-centered despite my best attempts — this is more about me than him,
as I have ever seen

writing as an inherently selfish act, turning inward, to the way which I
experience loss, mourn my past, fear my own death,

and this is the part of the Ghazal that I realize this ancient form
means nothing to me,

here, today, sitting in my apartment in Brooklyn,
nowhere near the sands of Syria
having learned to read with Yeats and Eliot and Pound,
not
        the sufi mystics and their tragic,
                              divine love
a child of the violence of Modernist free-verse,
the messy sprawl of
                words and empty space
and none of the solid, reassurance
that comes
        with
the calm, measured lines of
a Sonnet or Roundel

or this Ghazal for James, a stranger whose death strikes uncomfortably
close to home as I, Chris, lapsed poet, struggle to make an invisible death
forever seen.

A Ghazal for Jim Foley
C.S. Carrier

I am a carrier of light—Yo canto su elegancia con palabras que gimen
to bear him into the present—a poetic offering for Jim Foley.

A sorrow breaking "the balconies open" and his "qasidas braided,
on the horizon"—a heart irisaba de agonía writing for Jim Foley.

A guerrilla action against the minotaurs' sludgy gaze—a fiery lilac,
an unruly ghazal in "language not Arabic"—singing for Jim Foley.

Amidst a "madness of the desert"—las campanas de arsénico y el humo
a state of "prayers in Arabic"—a lost homecoming for Jim Foley.

Kneeling in an orange jumpsuit with light in his face—una frente
donde los sueños gimen—a shadow's sentence unfurling for Jim Foley.

I will not see his body laid out—but birds shredding the grass
trees and flowers wilting—a host of lands blistering for Jim Foley.

A life bruised and desolated by mad caliphs' madding verses
¡Que no quiero verla!—a blinding threshold opening for Jim Foley.

A "fire of men and stones" I say—an incendiary rain upon them,
a chorus of calls for forgiveness—a proper honoring for Jim Foley.

But, absolution attends forgiveness—and so instead I pity them
until they may spring un llanto como un río—raging for Jim Foley.

A desk in Arkansas—a window onto memory caked with salt
a las cinco de la tarde—a "language of loss" kindling for Jim Foley.

A presence in the field—a smile—un nardo / de sal y de inteligencia
a bridge crossing the ether—a kind of rendering for Jim Foley,

who attacks the rim and the dance floor and teaches a language
who drinks coffee under a tree—and writes—living for Jim Foley,

who in tactical vest and aviator shades—a chin to bear witness
¡Qué gran torero en la plaza!—cosmic scales iridescing for Jim Foley.

Ghazal of Witness

Daniel Mahoney

It's hard to believe the arc of history bends toward justice when history
repeats every five minutes and Justice is just a girl's name. Fix

yourself to the screen, try not to scream: we wrack, we catch ourselves,
then hang ourselves instead of our hats. Did you hear? The passengers are
sick!

The moon's a dead white fish! Did you hear they killed Lorca? Hung a sign
that said he was here until he wasn't, here until the fascists

killed him. They said: mariposa...mariposa....mariposa. Which means
butterfly or faggot in Spanish. His sister got a call in Madrid, said diga, which

means tell me or hello, then Lorca's body fell dead through the phone.
My heart... Jim, your face just now.... This is not the end of it....

Tyndale built his English bible from the original Hebrew & Greek,
so the church killed him twice: strangled, then burned him. History
is witness.

We see through a glass, darkly, and we write to take a swing at the darkness.
The King James Bible is Tyndale; he lives in lines writers have ripped

for centuries. O brother, dear brother. We steal, we beg and borrow.
We burrow, go toe-to-toe, looking for truth because... Because Nazim
Hikmet

said, the point is never to surrender. If history is a lake of fire, a screen
on some kid's Gameboy, then we are witness to rain, the very sun's a gift,

and nothing is finished. The sun still shines on the hill where they killed you
and the rain will never stop falling, even when we feel nothing but distance.

Jim, I have to tell you, when I saw you on the screen I didn't know, until
I knew. And your body fell through me like rain. And then the endless abyss.

A day later I brought my son to the cabin in Maine. You remember? He sat
where you sat looking out to sea. His body a furious abundance, a drift

of your body, his face your face. And that was all. You are no further from
me than your work, growing as my son grows from the living truth of it.

These are the names: Lorca, Hikmet, Tyndale, Foley. Their words
speak louder than their deaths. Their work is a ministry of witness.

Bad Sufi Feeling

Claire Morgana Gillis

I've got a bad Sufi feeling,
he says,
my translator in Baghdad.
(We should have gone together.)

It feels like?
When the lightning strikes
When the Maghrib sounds.

There's something about dusk,
he says,
my Sufi translator.
Brings out the Jinns,
he says.

Some are good and some are
not.
They tempt people,
and distract them as they make their way home.

You were taken in the hour of the Jinns,
Jim –
It was November, dark and cold.
(We should be drinking beers together, right now.)

I've got a bad Sufi feeling, Jim.
That road – those trees –
The light shifting in the mountains –

Don't go, Jim.
Please don't go.

It was a Thursday,
and you were on your way home.

Jim, I have a bad Sufi feeling.

GHAZAL [JIM]
Ethan Paquin

In a poem like this, embered reflection, to bring up the stirring of dust
would be too obvious – yet, in my eyes, the perpetual whirring of dust

and the scattering of pages in wind, nearby a Brutalist University Hall
else a bunch of nowhere dunes wherein you prayed, I'm sure. Cling of dust

to your handsome face, sandy hair and far-off eyes, studying the texture
of dreamscape memories of Cura and Chris and Noy, ever blurring. Of dust

we are, to dust shall we go, volumes high in the scarcely-lit stacks of DuBois
slightly dust-meagred but there, always there, those ideas demurring of dust

and of musty prose clichés but rather exploring, seeking into, as I knew you
always did through care and inquisition into wherever you were. Ring of dust

orbiting around my now middle-aged cortex of dashed lines, I still hear
you and we're young men. In your manuscript: desert reportage occurring
(of dust,

even then, you seemed enamored; to the sands even then you seemed
destined, sands of everywhere/anywhere a story was had), passages referring
of dust

and of far-flung characters and lives. You cared, you looked, you always saw,
friend, always did. That's what we remember – you're the defleuring of dust

from this sad mantle; you're a revealer of life. Ethan and Yago and _____
all store this within: the face of the handsome journeyer, the abjuring of dust.
FoleyBook_

The Blue Sea Seemed Further Than It Was
Yaddyra Peralta

This brown horizon a mirage of boundaries
as large as the foam on the surface of the sea.

Of the seas we are, salty in your lonely hours,
of stilled air, of all-silence and grief not of the sea.

And which of us knows the heat of Christ's temptations,
days as endless as the endlessness of the seas.

Breath stone, night black, breathe fire and sand, and sweat. Free fall:
where firmament, where grass, why this carpet, not the sea?

A bead, a bead, dry mouth, a bead, and breath, a bead,
your skin, skin of humanity, shore of what sea.

Stilled air, stilled air, the hush of harshness and open eyes.
There, on the wall, a lost bird, looking for the sea.

Ghazal for a Tall Boy From New Hampshire
Martín Espada

—For Jim Foley, journalist beheaded on video by ISIS, August 19, 2014

The reporters called and asked me: Did you know him?
I was his teacher, I said many times that day. Yes, I knew him.

Once he was a teacher too, teaching in another mill town
where the mills have disappeared. There, they knew him.

He taught the refugees from an island where the landlords
left them nothing but their hands. In Spanish, they knew him.

They sounded out the English, made the crippled letters
walk across the page for him, all because they knew him.

He ate their rice and beans, held their infants, posed with them
for snapshots at the graduation. Ask them how they knew him.

Beliza, Mónica, Limary: with him they wrote a poem of waterfalls
and frogs that sing at night, so he could know them as they knew him.

We know his words turn to rain in the rain forest of the poem.
We cannot say what words are his, even though we knew him.

His face on the front page sold the newspapers in the checkout line.
His executioners and his president spoke of him as if they knew him.

The reporter with the camera asked me if I saw the video his killers
wanted us to see. I muttered through a cage of teeth: No. I knew him.

Once he was a tall boy from New Hampshire, standing in my doorway.
He spoke Spanish. He wanted to teach. I knew him. I never knew him.

Rt. 25, Indiana
Ben Balthaser

I didn't know these cornfields were once a massacre: a plaque
to the dead children of the Potowatomie, as if a rock could remember

what we have forgotten. On the shredded edge of this country road,
I hear a Senator say on the radio we are dropping bombs to remember

Jim's name. There is the silence in the aftershock of the rifle
shot, when even the trees shed their dust, as if they could remember

what it was like to be surprised by pain. In the shallow of a drainage
ditch, I am startled by this frank boulder, as if we could re-member

bodies by claiming the earth over which they were torn open: the swept
plain of red and yellow Cargill triangles warning of pesticide: what could we remember

in such a place? The first time I knew what an explosion felt like
I was 17, my mother slumped over the wheel, trying to remember

her name, while the shattered glass fell about my knees as if the sky could
break open: I ran from the car and into the oncoming traffic, unable to remember

that death comes as often from our leaps to freedom. Jim, you
deserve something better than this, you mark the moment we remember

what it means to mourn our incompleteness. In a field much like this one
I imagine the white, distant vapor trails as war follows us inside memories

of our still-whole bodies, the urge to go where we want, now a Senator's
bomb, or a monument radiant under lights: what we build when we have
nothing left to remember.

Poem 52: for Jim Foley
Andew Varnon

"Beheaded," I heard
on the radio in Canada,
driving home.

New York tabloids
stamp your name
in dark Helvetica.

Your death tells us
everything they think
we need to know
about Syria.

Scrubbing the floor,
the rag I'm using was once
a T-shirt; it reads
"UMass Basketball."

Once, I hit the shot
on the floor at half-time
and climbed back up the stands
to high fives with all the guys.

Basketball, Boyden gym:
the gray standard-issue shorts
we wore then, writers
on the pick and roll.

You were fiction, I
was poetry. Our paths hardly
crossed. Only after grad school,
journalism called us both.
I went local and you, global.

In the newspapers now, you
are always wearing aviator shades,
flak jackets. In my memory, you
always had a square jaw, perpetual
shadow, that deep, gentle voice.

I didn't know
you that well,
I didn't know
we were almost
the same age,
I didn't know
I should have been
paying attention
to the number of days
gone missing, to
the blue mosque door,
the Arabic graffiti on the walls,
the labyrinth of bombed out buildings
and rubble, the sound
you hear in the turret
when you take fire.

For you, I'd like to drink away
the deadlines at father's hours
at a bar in a sleepy town.

I'm convinced, no,
I've convinced myself you
were there, and I

I gave you five.

Illocution & Colors

Rachelle Linda Escamilla

Could the sky be any color if the word for blue is ?
The color of my skin in Mandarin is red, brown is absent.

The field full of brassicas is green beneath the missing water mountains.
My home a poemdry dirt beneath resting bodies: faces omitted.

Neon orange street signs   dayglo pink hotpants   bodies of colors
walking in malls
bodies of bodies picking   stories omitted.

Whose bodies enbrowned?
Skylines beyond too gold   hillsides water omitted.

How do I tell you the color of China, if colors in China are GONE
the feeling of fuchsia, hardplasticblue sandals: a tenuous rainbow.

Teach a child the star twinkles and it does, tell her it's blue   the sky:
whose omitted story, like the bodies of brown workers, exists.

Christmas Poem for Jim Foley
Mike Dockins

For you, Foley, a simple Coca-Cola,
poured from an ice-cold can over ice & splashed
with lime. A gaggle of nephews, nieces—
why not a few neighborhood urchins—crashing
through the house strumming their new toys:
globes & zeppelins (wow, a zeppelin!) & NERF
guns & skateboards & crayons & aluminum bats
& gyrobots & ukuleles & toy helicopters.
A simple pop melody jangling along the ceiling.
For you, a story, a dream, to chase, to catch.
An old dog with milk-mouth to paw at you
because he can't get enough scratches under his chin,
& because who knows how much time he has left,
& because who knows how much time any of us
have left inside our crackable piggy banks
of Time. For you, to be surrounded by folks
who adore you—hell, who merely tolerate you,
& everyone else can go fly their ignorant kites.
A D-major chord struck low on a pitch-perfect piano,
& you get to decide whether to switch to E-minor
or to G-Major, & after that, a brand-new song
that anticipates a brand-new year. For you, the sack
pulled off your head, the cuffs cracked, the blades
sheathed, the approaching roar of helicopters
jangling across the ceiling of the far-off sky.
For you, somebody, anybody, to say these things,
& maybe even to mail them someplace.
For you, thousands, millions—it's not unreasonable
to say billions—of people pinpricking this silly globe,
all of us wishing you a Merry Christmas, Jim.

Ghazal

Shauna Seliy

How to thank the Jesuits of Malta, you asked me to help craft a letter.
They'd prayed for you in your first captivity, you'll remember.

You had a glass of water, the baby chewed your watch, then you
vanished forever. Did I take you to the train? Say a serious goodbye?
I don't remember.

Walking with me into class, into parties, into bars, for years, remember?
Next to me, in movie theaters, libraries, cars. I wonder if you remember.

We got lost, a winter afternoon, Logan Square, Lake Street, North Avenue.
We stood on some roof and looked at the skyline, one that maybe you'll
remember.

You kept up the spirits of the other prisoners, that's what they remember.
But where are you now, and in that wherever, can you even remember?

"I ask for the captors to have mercy," the prayer my sister made for you.
After they killed you, you came here, three loud birds in the tree next door,
remember?

"I remember you two in class," a friend says at your memorial. "You always
sat together."
Your laugh, so distinctive and loud, but how long will I remember?

I can't hear my name said in your voice. Did you ever call me Shauna?
S.S. Dude. Sister. Sweetie. Chica. For now, those are the words I remember.

In the Absence of Sparrows *

Daniel Johnson

Rockets concuss. Guns rattle off.
Dogs in a public square
feed on dead horses.

I don't know, Jim, where you are.
When did you last see
birds? The winter sky in Boston

is gray with flu. Newspapers,
senators, friends, even your mom
on Good Morning America—

no one knows where you are.
It's night, cold and bruised,
where you are. Plastic twine binds

your hands. You wait and pray, pray
and wait, but this is where the picture goes gray.
We don't know, Jim, where you are.

*

In the absence of sparrows: a crowd of friends and family gather in Rochester,
New Hampshire to recite the holy rosary.

*

We keep your picture on the kitchen table, pack of American Spirits,
airplane bottle of Scotch, a copy of Krapp's Last Tape.

Don't get me wrong; we expect you back. Skinny, feral,
coffee eyes sunken but alive, you've always come back, from Iraq,

Syria, Afghanistan, even Libya after Gaddafi's forces
captured and held you for 44 days. You tracked time scratching

marks with your zipper on prison walls, scrawling notes on cigarette
boxes, reciting the Koran with other prisoners. Then, you called.

DJ, it's Jimmy…I'm in New Hampshire, brother! I wanted
to break your fucking nose. We ate lobster rolls, instead,

on a picnic bench by Boston Harbor. You made a quick round
of TV shows, packed your camera and Arabic phrasebook.

You skipped town on a plane to Turkey. We talked once. You said
you'd play it safe. The connection was lost.

*

In the absence of sparrows: American journalist James Foley disappeared
after being taken captive by armed gunmen near Aleppo, Syria on
Thanksgiving Day.

In the absence of sparrows: our house burns blue with news.

*

Winter solstice, 1991. You turned donuts,
drinking beers, in a snowy public lot next to the lake.
Girls yelped. You cranked the Pixies louder, cut the lights,
and steered Billy's grandma's Chrysler onto the Winnipesaukee ice.
The moon flamed bright as a county coroner's light.
You revved the station wagon's engine. Billy tied
a yellow ski rope off the hitch, flashed a thumbs up,
and you punched the gas—5, 15, 20, 25 miles per hour—
towing Billy, skating in high-top sneakers,
across the frozen lake. Chill air filled his lungs.
Billy pumped his fist. You torqued the wheel left.
Triumphant, you honked and flashed the lights.
You took a swig of Heineken and wheeled
the wood-paneled station wagon in a wide-arcing turn
to pick up Billy, bloodied but standing. People do reckless things
but your friends dubbed you the High King of Foolish Shit.
The nose of Billy's grandma's Chrysler broke the ice.
You jammed it into reverse. Bald tires spinning,
you flung yourself from the car. In seconds, it was gone.
You gave Billy's grandma a potted mum
and a silver balloon. Standing on her screened-in porch,
you mumbled an apology. What am I supposed to do now?

she asked. What the hell do I do now?

*

In the absence of sparrows: when falling snow, out the window, looks like
radio waves, your face appears, your baritone laugh.

*

August 31, 2004

We read Abbie Hoffman, 1968, watched Panther documentaries,
The Weather Underground, and packed our bandanas, first aid kits,
fat markers, maps and signs for New York City. A31, they called it,
a day of direct action, a time to heave ourselves on the gears

of an odious machine. We marched, drumming and chanting, half a million
strong, through the streets of Lower Manhattan. Worst President Ever,
A Texas Village Has Lost Its Idiot. Protestors carried a flotilla of flag-covered
coffins. We hoisted homemade signs and cried out, Whose streets?

Our streets? No justice, no peace! I'd packed sandwiches,
water, mapped restrooms along the parade route, inked
the hotline for Legal Services on your forearm and mine.
You, my wild half brother, packed only a one hitter, notepad, and pen.

When the parade snaked past the New York Public Library,
we peeled off to confront 20 cops in riot gear blocking entry
with batons drawn. We took position on the library steps.
Stone-still, inches from police, we held our signs

stamped with a student gagged by padlock and chain.
I could feel breath on my neck. We narrowly escaped arrest,
then streamed toward the Garden, a ragtag troop of 200.
We evaded barricades. Cut down alleys. At Herald Square, only

blocks from the Republican Convention, cops on mopeds
cut us off. They rolled out a bright orange snow fence,
hundreds of yard long, then zip cuffed us, one by one.
I called Ebele. You called your brother, set to be married in just three days.

His best man, you were headed to jail. "I'll be there Friday for the golf outing,"
you vowed, a cop cutting your phone call short. They took you first.
Threw you on a city bus headed to Pier 14 on the Hudson,
a giant garage stinking of axel grease and gasoline. Stepping off the bus,

I scanned hundreds of faces staring through chain link, newly erected
and topped with concertina wire. I couldn't find you. I can't. They transferred
me, in soapy light, to the Tombs, Manhattan's city jail, and freed me after
24 hours to wander the streets. I peered in Chinese restaurants, seedy
Canal Street bars,

called your cell phone from a payphone, trekked to Yago's apartment
in Spanish Harlem, eager to crack beers, to begin weaving the story
we would always tell. You were not there. Waiting outside the Tombs,
I missed my flight home. Waiting, I smoked your cigarettes on the fire escape.

They held you and held you. You are missing still. I want to hold you. Beauty
is in the streets, my brother. Beauty is in the streets.

*

In the absence of sparrows: trash fires, a call to prayer. Dusk.
Rockets whistling, plastic bags taking flight.

In the absence of sparrows: all of a sudden, you appear. Standing before a
cinder block wall, you're holding a video camera with a boom mic and
wearing a bulletproof vest.

In the absence of sparrows: the front page story says you've been missing
since November 22, 2012. Everything else it doesn't say.

In the absence of sparrows: you simply wandered off, past the Sunoco,
pockets stuffed. The door to your apartment is open still—

© 2014 Daniel Johnson. Distributed by King Features Syndicate
*Originally published in electronic form on the website for POEM-A-DAY:
New and Classic Poems Provided by the Academy of American Poets.

Compound Memorandum
James Foley

> — "All the archetypes of dysfunction, disease and disuse are found on the compound." –Anonymous

Subject: Compound Memorandum
Re: The compound is outfitted for projects that have been established to bring the goodwill and expertise from one country to a smaller country that was ripped apart when the larger country invaded for the purpose of bringing freedom to the smaller country's people. (The names of which have been withheld to prevent legal action by one country's offices, per gag order, against writer who may or may not still be employed with the office.)

It is a small compound, approximately three and a half city blocks of street walled in of what was once a posh neighborhood, now a series of dead ends and abandoned embassies, controlled by religious men wielding semi-automatic weapons. And across the street from one of the world's largest uncompleted mosques, a project of the former strong man, a forest of abandoned cranes of various heights looming over the collapsed domes.

A compound guarded by mercenaries from a southern hemisphere country, who speak a guttural, continental-sounding language, carry machine guns that shoot a large caliber bullet, and who ferry clients in four-door vehicles outfitted with heavier springs to support added tonnages.

Their clients, a class of advisor experienced in countries rated high-conflict, i.e. consultants who specialize in extreme zones, places which the global first world refer to as hell- holes, but known to be lucrative, to the tune of two-thirds danger pay to an amended contract, all billable by the contractor to the occupying gov't.

Heretofore referred to as the partner government, the purpose of this document being not to shine a light on practices of over-billing, or tax-payer waste, but rather to present the realities of how the individuals, a percentage of who speak the native language and hold western passports, interact in such a fishbowl.

Which is precisely a compound divided by one irregularly-paved, one lane boulevard, between concrete T-Walls—twelve feet high, three feet thick—1,400 footsteps from guarded gate to guarded gate, with a crossroads at one end where the armored vehicles enter and exit in three-vehicle convoys.

A neighborhood within the neighborhood, villas topped by guard positions, outside of which exists an actual city, the vastness of which can only be captured by guards atop the shattered intelligence headquarters. A city, once possibly the world's most dangerous and yet inside, with one of the highest ratios of guards to civilians, possibly the most secure, pierced at dawn and dusk by the simultaneous calls to prayer, and the daily rotor thwock of helicopters.

Arrival of the Correspondent
To this compound arrived a reporter who had come from covering the conflict zone outside. At the time of his arrival, he had a shaved head, wore cargo pants and boots, as if he was a member of the military unit with whom he had been embedded, meaning sitting in the back of armored vehicles as they rolled up and down the northern trash-strewn highways escorting fuel convoys and following on patrols through neighborhoods of the former dictator's sect.

He wore the same footwear as soldiers, in order to report on their activities, when in fact he had no military experience, and he was more youngish looking than his years indicated, and now, on the compound, eager to please to the extent to cover his own lack of experience in this line of communications and public relations work.

A reporter who knew he'd compromised his writer's integrity to get the job, but who was also completely buried in debt, chalked to grad school, but also to the pursuit of certain kind of assignments, such that the war zone had provided for the previous six months.

Who took an identity as a war correspondent by virtue of a single incident, having witnessed the aftermath of a car bombing, the now indelible images of a well-dressed woman wearing a hijab and matching dress limping past soldiers, still clutching her purse, one hand covering half her chin, two cars on fire in the background, an armored jeep thrown sideways in the middle of the street, a ten-foot crater in front, bodies being pulled from the rubble that had fallen on the flaming cars, and the intermittent noise of local soldiers firing AK-47s down empty alleyways.

And the feeling not of horror or disgust, but a rush, the kind of Gatling gun of endorphins of which he'd never experienced even on his best artificially induced or thrill-seeking trip, still streaming through him hours later in the hangar-sized chow hall, with the memorial to thirteen dead when another suicide attacker blew himself up inside, years earlier.

A rare high from the momentary proximity to death, after six months of waiting for it, although he wouldn't have admitted this to anyone, and he still completed his HR packetand emailed it to the contracting company based in the capital, acknowledging in some sense, that for him at least, the war was over.

Air-Conditioning
And at first he had difficulty sleeping in a queen-sized bed in his air-conditioned room on the compound because he was used to the aluminum trailer units that at least two soldiers occupied, sometimes four, and this was a room with grand bureaus, with a king-sized bed and a maid service to fold his clothes and make his bed.

Texas T-Wall
Of information useful to compound dwellers: The Texas T-wall is 12 feet high, blast protection height being calculated as the cube root, in feet, of the explosive weight, in pounds of T.N.T., therefore; the blast from a thousand-pound suicide car bomb, a large size for a car, if it exploded next to the wall, would need at least 10 feet of height to absorb it.

The extra two feet for peace of mind, added to the cost, being 300 dollars per unit, percentages for neighboring concrete magnates pouring the $300 pedestals into molds, which when hardened and raised, somehow reminded the reporter of Easter Island totems—but faceless—the rows of which tightened into concentric circles in the center of the city known as the Green Zone, where the partner and occupied governments' held their offices.

Contraband Substances
Through the partner country's postal system, established for the hundred thousand odd soldiers deployed to the country, the reporter received some substances sealed in a bag of coffee and smoked the substances, and listened to their man wailing music and wrote in a notebook, and when he fell asleep, inadvertently saw himself falling through a strung soup of Arabic symbols and glottal stops.

And just before waking, the reporter saw a bird's eye view of the compound, of the labyrinth of valves and neighborhood stop gates sealing off certain streets and alleyways from the broader, yet broken streets around it. And, as if his eyes encompassed the bank of black and white screens in the cigarette-stained surveillance room, the cameras caught views of dozens of angles and blind corners.

On the upper left screen, a battered taxi with a gray body and an orange door pulling to the front gate,
and out of it a girl with a covered head, wearing a colorful cocoon of long skirts and wraps, with an attention to detail that impressed everyone, and who foreigners observed must have spent a bundle, the bulk of her salary, on her appearance.

A girl who worked as a collaborator, as the locals say, a label then difficult to navigate, but not common knowledge with respect to her, thankfully, as it would have presented a serious problem should anybody in her neighborhood, least of all her brothers, possess this information.

Brothers who had certain opinions, established during the height of bad times, after one of the brothers, the one who had set out to be an oil products engineer and who had become a carp farmer, was forced to lie on the ground when forces of the occupiers entered their house in a former shopping district and the boot of one of the occupiers crushed one of his eyeglass lenses, which at that time could not be replaced, while the better seeing brother stood in a corner being sniffed at by a bomb dog, as the occupiers' eyes shielded by dark sunglasses, looked sideways at their sister and exchanged foreign words.

And although neither brother spoke the occupiers' tongue, this proved to be a defining incident, after which the brothers held things for a party of men who the occupiers were always looking for.

Partner Country Assistance

But, she liked working for the partner country's program, and working in an office where she had her own desk and computer, and internet, and where her boss, a director of monitoring and evaluation from the southern continent, a father of four and a Pentecostal with a fondness for Absolut Vodka, mock-scolded her like her father would have.

She, entering data on her laptop with several online chats opened simultaneously, her nails painted in silver sparkles, reminding one of the dictator's mirrored, mostly shattered chandeliers, in palaces now mostly being cleared of the partner country's military brass to make way for reoccupation by the country's own officials.

However, she would be moved to another department as requested by another senior advisor who called for her administrative help, specifically. A request to which the chief of party, a former Ivy League professor and anthropologist, who viewed the rivalries between respective advisors and their personal fiefdoms with a certain anthropological detachment, and whose philosophy was not to intervene until personal attacks increased in the form of copy-all emails of the sort that embarrassed the home office, was reluctant not to grant, as the advisor had recently scored a major coup with the Council of Ministers.

All unbeknownst to the girl as she stepped through the outer compound gate manned by former militants from the neighborhood, passed through the staggered inner T-Walls and second gate manned by the subcontinental's machine gun nest, and into the corridor of T-Walls, in between which the luxury villas, where the expatriates alternatively lived and worked, were ensconced, and where the locals served as tea boys, maids, runabouts, data entry specialists and in increasing cases, as advisors themselves.

She passed the boys in blue uniforms watering the walkways, soaking the ever-present dust blown in brown clouds from the desiccated plains where there was no longer enough river or rain to keep the fields from crumbling, past the maids with head coverings of less expensive cloth, who collected the clients' towels and laundry and steamed them in vats of commercial soap that caused rashes among several, until enough complaints were filed.

And the transferal of the girl's computer, her pillow-covered Kleenex box and framed picture of the cartoon boy and girl in love, to the office of the senior advisor, a lawyer disparaged by some as a tax clerk, and universally rumored to be a steerer of contracts, as was paramount to greasing the wheels with the recipient government, but also the architect of a wide-reaching civil service law that might stretch reform across the blighted land if only the law would be enacted by the Council of Ministers before the upcoming election, when the power structure might well turn on its head or solidify in ways no one in the compound could predict.

The senior advisor's local advisor spoke to her of the prestige of being transferred to such a department. She nodded mechanically, and noticed her ex-boss's look as she exited her new boss's office at the end of the day, to the battered taxi waiting at the end of the compound that ferried her back to her brothers who were having trouble finding work of their own, and didn't need to hear that she'd lost her job at the Ministry of Trade, where she told them she was working.

Waking Life on the Compound
And the reporter would eventually wake to a neighbor, a senior foreign investments advisor lamenting a lost or stolen I-Pod, and believe it was the moaning of the woman with shrapnel embedded in her chin, and upon fully waking, realize it wasn't, and take two Aspirin, chug a bottle of water and ultimately sit at his desk and begin writing the project's overdue success stories.

Reworking sentences of haphazard technical language and jumbled punctuation, his compound duties punctuated by the occasional rumblings from the sectarian beast in the form of fertilizer packed flat-beds or mini-buses detonating into government offices, splintering hundreds with shattered glass, making sandwiches of the still living until blood collected in puddles as if from open pipes. The biggest concussions of which demanded the answering of emails from families who'd seen such horrific scenes on cable news, which the compound dwellers sometimes pre-empted with status updates such as, I'm Ok.

The reporter was given assignments to write success stories on the project outreaches and accomplishments, such as to deliver video conference equipment where there was a dearth of bandwidth, or strategic communications strategies to a department from which a director was a former assassin of employees, of a different sect, now brought back into the fold; not to take an inherently antagonistic tone to such assistance which indeed trained thousands of ministry employees and certainly filled some with a small hope for the future, if only the power structure would allow change to flower from within the technocracy, which couldn't authentically be posited until the partner country and its entire portfolio left the host country, as in helicopters on rooftops, not the official pretenses thereof.

At times compound doors slammed and the locals jumped in their skin as if they'd heard bombs detonating, and at other times, actual bombs detonated and the advisors glanced casually as if doors were slammed, the blaséness of which the reporter believed amounted to a certain posturing, as the majority of advisors had not experienced much outside the compound, except those who'd escaped the country some decades prior and now percentages rode around in armored convoys like the rest.

And the reporter wondered if he really wished he could run out and interview and take pictures of the ripped open bodies and gashes that poured out of the line of people running from the smoking wreckages of flipped and twisted automotive parts, or did he just wish that he wished it.

He wondered whether he'd become inured to the pain of these people, isolated in their country as if forever caught on a desert island, from which only the wealthiest could slip, cross cut by currents, due to diplomatic differences by which almost no visas were granted, wading dangerously close to faceless hands that snagged ankles, bound hands, yanked a cousin or schoolmate from a hospital bed into the maelstrom where a drill bit might be pressed through the cerebellum. Transforming a body into a corpse floating on their Biblical river, a condition the local police were reluctant to retrieve unless it floated toward a particular bank—waiting instead for the occupying forces to use a particular hook to ease it towards the bank.

A body bloated into a dark and inflatable shape, or perhaps not misshapen, merely disappeared into a haphazardly dug pit with no record of, as newspapers were almost exclusively party mouthpieces, not the burgeoning fourth estate the partner country had hoped to establish by propping up alternative TV and radio stations.

Special Immigrant Visa

The reporter took up the study of Arabic and dropped it a month later when he realized there would never be a chance to use it outside the walls, the agreement between security contractor and project not permitting any visits, personal or touristic, beyond going to and from project meetings and conferences, not counting visits to the bottle store, known euphemistically as, The Pharmacy.

Nor did he believe he would ever visit this country of his own accord, nor did he want to. He too could disappear forever, he reminded himself. He had a passport, a reserved plane ticket, which reminded him of his choices, and the reason why many of the locals risked their lives to work on the compound, precisely for the Special Immigrant Visa.

Which in exchange for one calendar year's worth of work with a partner governmental agency, granted a chance to leave the semblance of a republic for the perceived paradise of the partner nation via a lengthy application process.

An idea inspired by images emailed by former colleagues posing outside a steak house insome southwestern city, embracing wife and daughter, in front of a newish model SUV, a lit sidewalk, unmarred by trash or sewage in the background, as if one could half grant oneself new citizenship by dreaming oneself into such pictures.

The girl too dreamed, and of yes, brand-named cosmetics, Channel sunglasses and shoes from Nordstrom's, and more importantly, of leaving her brothers not as a married woman, but perhaps in the middle of the night, perhaps to say goodbye over the phone as they screamed at her, bound for a city of lights, which didn't suddenly cut, a city not necessarily of Hollywood stars, but out of which floated a certain sheen of new bed sheets, huge sunrises, of outlaws crashing through police blockades in stolen cars, and emerald colored swimming pools. So she had joined the cue of those applying.

New Boss
Her new boss, the senior advisor, known for well-pressed shirts, golfing hats and his general ignoring of others as he strolled the compound's boulevard, had been working in the war-torn country for close to five years, considered an insane amount of time to be away from a wife and two young boys, and disconnected from normalcy, whether of the Burger King, mega-mall or walking in the woods variety.

The suspicion being he hated his wife, which fit with his reputation for desiring of proximity to young office girls, not that this was anything new, the compound retaining the whiff of gender roles germane to ex-dictatorships, sheikdoms, and for an attractive girl, a life beyond pure survival.

She did her work, mostly arranging the distribution of the new draft law to Provincial Council centers and making follow up calls to ensure they received it. He called her work excellent, which she didn't believe, since he spoke the regional language too, and all she'd done was make some phone calls using a respectful tone, and the locals said all these projects did anyways, was steal, since a quarter of every million went to the ones who wore the bullet proof and carried guns, a quarter to foreign salaries, over a quarter to various party pockets, and whatever was left to the people it was intended for.

And there was an opaqueness to the thoughts behind the panes of the senior advisor's prescription glasses, as he reiterated that he needed someone who could work irregular hours, who could take trips to the provinces, also possibly abroad. She explained, perhaps revealing too much, that she needed to explain it to her brothers first.

But, at 3:50 on her second day, he requested she stay an extra hour, as if testing her, as if she would or wouldn't, and she replied, of course, as long as she called the driver of her battered taxi, and at 4:50, he asked if she would stay a second hour.(full disclosure: The reporter has a vested interested in the details of this particular tangent, however he doesn't speak the language and therefore is precluded from understanding many, probably more intimate details of the narrative, which took place on the compound during his tenure there.)

Provincial Trip
A month later the advisor secured two tickets to go to the northern most province of the country, the province which happened to be the most stable, and also the home of its own oppressed ethnic group, now seeking independence from former ruling groups. A province which had its shit together, so to speak, and therefore maintained almost regular electricity, foreign development projects, take-out restaurants, commercial hotels- any three of which boasted better quality services than the overpriced, 80's style behemoth inside the beleaguered capital, which charged exorbitant buffet prices and often lacked, say, quality toilet paper.

She told her brothers she'd been selected by her ministry supervisor to attend the international conference in a neighboring capitol. She went as far as to enlist her friend, the one with the graphic design software, to print a fake invitation, not entailing the levels of guilt this required. Her brothers approved, as long as she promised not to go anywhere in the capitol at night, infidels and fornicators were everywhere, as was well-known.

And so she went to the airport, guarded by three outer checkpoints and passed her mother's old buckle suitcase through five metal detectors. The first time she'd been to the airport since when her father took them to the region's mega-city and she remembered skyscrapers shaped like Transformers and the stick-legged, pink-feathered birds and salt and sand beaches, and running and skinning her knee to see a statue of four bronze horses galloping out of a bronze sea, and of a certain styrofoam seahorse her father had bought her, that she'd kept in her bed always, until the time they had to leave their house in the middle of the night.

The girl and the advisor boarded the plane, and the blond stewardesses spoke another language, even though the steel tail proclaimed the logo of their own battered country, but inside it smelled of new carpet and plastic seats, and they were served cans of orange or grape soda and packaged sweets, and for some reason when the senior advisor put his tray down to receive his soda, he put his hand under her tray and squeezed the top of her knee, and then the middle of her thigh, and her leg popped like the top of the aspirin bottle, knocking his soda onto his pants, coursing forth with fizz.

One word escaped his mouth as he used a Kleenex to dab at the orange stain on his lap, as the plane took off, to a turbulence of stomach and head, until she believed she would vomit or die, and so froze herself to survive.

But 45 minutes later, they landed to fresher, lighter air and were whisked by taxi to a conference center with sparkling floors, high ceilings painted to look like abstract clouds and meetings with drab officials, somehow twice as tolerable, and oh, of a hotel whose sheets smelled of a scented breeze and an Asian restaurant staffed by real Asians.

Vengeful Fires

The advisor forewent another meeting and asked her to dinner on the ninth floor, still wearing his suit, and she of still unsettled stomach, but also wearing earrings and no hijab, smiled weakly.

Large windows reflected her curls by candlelight. She didn't know what to say. It was all very strange, sitting across from a boss who might reach out and grab her again, and who knew what she would or wouldn't do if he tried. What a mistake to travel with him just so she could travel! A mistake, terrible.

He looked at her flatly, and her stomach began to seep acid. He uncorked a bottle of wine. She didn't partake. He leaned across the white table cloth, and began, speaking of the birth of his youngest child, of seeing his wife, sweaty, holding her reddened son in her arms, victorious after an all night struggle in the hospital, his son's hair preternaturally thick with eyes of the just born blue gray, starring out, perhaps blindly, at this new wide world, except that it sounded better in the language he spoke to her of it.

Beautiful images, confused somewhat, when he came into her room later that night, not knowing how he got a key card and also strange that he did not say, may I come in, even though, that would have given her the opportunity to refuse him.

She could see his shining spectacles like round mirrors in the darkness, as he laid them on the bed stand and the soft sagging sound of the cushion as he laid down beside her on the double bed. And then, he turned in the motion of an athlete catching a ball, as she turned and faced the wall, and he took her from behind in his arms. And, she held her breath as if holding it signified she wasn't there. He spoke in her ear that he'd wanted to hold her since their first meeting—that he had to protect her from the jealous ones.

She said nothing, as she tried to breathe, not smell the cologne on his neck, imagining instead the items her brothers had once held for the militia in the long box under the floor boards under their parent's old bed, tubes the older once assembled by moonlight to show her. Her brothers now aiming them at the hotel bed, the whoosh of gasses released, to vengeful fires.

And at the same moment he reached down with both hands, and she held fast to the fastener of her jeans and pulled herself further towards the wall, as his hands rose again and felt the points of her breasts through the cotton gown, and she wrapped herself with her arms over his hands, and not being able to pry his hands away, began to get dizzy on the smell of him and, she turned, clamped her teeth against the shiny of the shirt in his under arm—the man odor—the shininess and the catch of her teeth, and she could do nothing but bite silently until he cried out, swung with an open hand, but missed her mouth, and withdrew, repeating an unrepeatable word. And the next morning they returned to the region's airport and then to the compound, with no chit-chat, and he ordered some assignments of her, no trace of the previous gentle nature in his voice.

Until a few mornings later, the girl's computer, her pillow shaped tissue box, and framed cartoon, were moved to a side office, little more than a utility closet where office supplies were kept, as an expression of the incompatibility of her presence in the senior advisor's working space, thus re-establishing the pattern whereby he acquired a new assistant, this time a 60-something, chain-smoking functionary from the Ministry of Defense, who he had no reason to fire, but whom he would.

Finding Meaning on the Compound

And the reporter, who has been slogging on his key board through the narratives- the surveying of broken canals, the installing of new statistical gathering software, despite hardware incompatibilities and/or electricity grid shortages, and the national government refusal of cooperation due to issues of sovereignty.

Interrupted by Thursday evenings dousing with pharmacy-bought cases of Absolut, in their compound bar named for the pink avian native to the southern region, while a replay of one of the partner country's sports events broadcast on the far flat screen, with an occasional raising a glass to the touch down, home run, three pointer, al-hum-du-la, al hum du la, to the blessings of the Almighty in the cadence of a professional sports mantra.

Alcohol being part of the adherence to a routine, a way to circumvent breakdown, emotional or otherwise, despite its propensity to do so, and so to pass time without feeling it so heavily, except on those mornings when he felt physically conscious of flushing his life down a semi-functioning pipe, until the Prime Minister's order to ban alcohol, seemed to interrupt, but had negligible effect on the compound's bar supply, due to pre-arranged measures.

Mirage Enters

And here, the reporter, fully close to a cycle whereby one decides to grow a slight paunch and order a gaming system, renews interest in the girl, as she is transferred, to the communications department, due to the intervention of his supervisor, a former journalist, who requested a native speaker to translate local press clippings.

The same communications director, who sometimes inserting her chin onto his shoulder as he typed, assigned him the bulk of success stories and flitted in and out of the office until one of the mercenaries strapped her bullet proof vest on crooked, throwing her back out, she claimed, after which she borrowed a bottle of pain killers from a former military intelligence officer, and began acting more erratically.

One of the consequences being, the reporter was the only one in the office the next day, and therefore, helped arrange the girl's computer, her tissue box and framed picture on the unoccupied desk, adjacent to his. He'd been told her name meant Mirage, by one of the senior advisor's assistants, and that she was problematic, not extremely reliable information, considering.

And when the director saw how the reporter had arranged the girl's desk, she accused him of undermining her authority, and he suggested she was paranoid. –Paranoid? she screamed. -Of what, you and that girl?

The reporter didn't reply, wondering if by Mirage, did her parents meant a vision, as she was neither extremely beautiful, for a woman from that city, nor extremely graceful, but she had a kind of hidden presence. Her clothes being colorfully elaborate, and yet chaste and yet just tight-fitting enough to be curvaceous, and he later learned she'd designed them herself.

And her eyes, her eyes held gravity's dark drops within lighter irises, possibly denoting a lineage that didn't involve the traditional arrangements between like sects, or the fact that she looked him directly in the eyes when he spoke to her.

And she spoke the partner country's tongue with a vaguely familiar lisp, the command of which derived from a specialization at the city's most recognized university, now overrun by young thugs, but more characteristic of online chatting, using words like cuz and bro. -Bro, she said, do you want coffee? As if she didn't know who she was saying it to, or had learned the words from a friend who'd worked with occupying soldiers.

And he nodded more out of embarrassment for her. And she went and made it for him, a rather bland Nescafe, instead of using the more proficient tea boy, because he couldn't tell if she was playing the deferential local, or making a play at him, which had previously happened on the compound, zero times, so that he felt out of practice.

And it was preferable to sip her instant coffee, write a few graphs of the latest request emailed from the communication director, until he spotted a yellow bubble on his screen requesting he confirm the girl as a chat friend.

He clicked yes, peripherally aware of her narrow face, lit bluish from the screen background, and framed by hijab, sometimes of a net, or a patterned cloth fabric, wrapped tightly around her head.
She was not extremely good looking, he decided, as with the large breasted maid who piously wiped down the bathroom sink as he was going to the shower each morning, but her total presence and attentiveness, combined with her sometimes seeming to day dream in his direction, as the communication's director was still mostly absent, felt as if invisible eyes were scanning him.

-Do you want to see my family cuz? -Cuz? What does Cuz mean? He replied. –Friend, don't it? –Sure it means friend, but not in the office environment, ok? -Ok, bro, an emoticon with googly eyes spiraled across the screen.

She sent him pictures of her family, her two brothers, one with large forehead frowning, the other the look of a junior professor with glasses, and her with curly hair sprung like a girl from the block in the partner nation's fashion capital, and she glanced at him, before she sent the file as if to decide if she trusted him, as if she was flipping off a switch in herself or defining a category for him, but so he could see her doing it.

-How was lunch, yummm? It pained him to answer these chats, as lunch was, in the same modified house cafeteria it was always in, as locals were not normally allowed, or when she routinely asked him if he needed anything outside, as if she couldn't understand that for him, there was no outside.

As in nothing fulfill able from outside, besides cigarettes, grilled plates and pirated DVDs, nothing that couldn't be ordered electronically of higher quality, but he started asking her for things, like packs of stale Marlboro Reds, that he gave to the static guards.

One day when she asked, he asked her for a pack of condoms, and she didn't reply, but he thought he saw her blush into her screen, so she knew what they were. And he decided to ask for her phone number. She scribbled it on a project Post-it, and passed it to him manually, but later chatted him extensively to ensure he wouldn't call until after she'd sent a text, indicating she was far enough out of her brothers' ear shots.

Late Night Phone
And so from infrequent phone calls to his late night dissection of all things on the compound, so she'd listen and to calibrate if she could respond intelligently, -So you want to leave, why you want to leave, bro? And, hearing that she had no idea what his life was like on the compound, nor he of hers outside, determined he could never seriously date her, but he continued to call to see what would happen if he did.

And imagining her listening with her lower half wrapped in blankets and upper in a sleeveless pink shirt he's seen in pictures, in an unheated room, with obviously poor cell reception, her asking him to stay on the phone as she fell asleep, infantile, but for the fact that it signaled almost sleeping with her, and so kept on about their over medicated boss, his dentist brother who continually asked him when he was coming home, and gossip about a certain senior advisor she was want to hear, and he -I wish you were with me right now, and she -I know, -what do you mean?

–I want to be there too, bro, –But what about what your parents would say? –I don't have any parents. –Sorry, what about your brothers? -I don't care what they say, they can't do anything.–You're the only who can do something, she said. I can, he said, but I can leave this country whenever.

She was quiet. –But at least I can see you tomorrow. At least I am here thinking about you.

It was the first time he thought maybe, that she was brave and smart. She had to be or pretend, and what was much of the difference in pretending and being if he felt it. Then he had an idea, and arranged for one of the locals who he trusted, the assistant to the chief of party, to acquire something for her, as in precious metals heavy on the limbs, the display of which still defined wealth, and this one had Onyx leopard spots encased in a face of gold dust, which cost him one eighth his monthly pay check, which was more than he had ever spent on a gift for anyone, even his mother.

And that day for lunch, he ordered a mixed grill of lamb, chicken, steak, including extra for the fat, and they sat at a lawn table in one of the gardens, which made her uncomfortable, as anyone could see they were having lunch together, alone.

-Why does it matter? he asked. Her eyes bulged, and he replied, –I want them to know. He had been thinking of this all night and had some robust beans for his coffee that morning. The sun was shining wide, the subcontinental peering down from the rooftop machine gun nest, possibly smiling wider. -But they will bother me if they know, she said.

–I got something for you, he took out the ring, the gold and leopard one, and she palm- over-heart as women worldwide were want to do to indicate they are temporarily touched beyond words.

The next day she wore the ring brazenly, telling her brothers it was a gift to herself, that she'd been saving for a year and a half, and they frowning at her capricious nature, but possibly impressed by her ability to save without decreasing what she was giving them.

On Giving in to Temptations

He walked her to the side gate where the locals exited in afternoons, and she almost not caring that eyes were looking, grabbed him above his elbow, whispering she wanted to give him something, looking the opposite way, meaning, he interpreted his villa, and so swung her swiftly, despite eyes watching them turn in front of the guard house where locals were patted down as they exited, mouths always ready to report on each other, and the cameras connected to the bank of screens, and hurrying her on this step forward.

And so in his room, with pulled shades, asked him to sit in his chair, and she removed it in one seemingly pulled motion, so it came apart in a long colored cloth, and tussled her hair with her ring hand until the curls emerged, like living coils, a few even blond, as in some dated nod to punk.

She smiling crookedly at his widening face. He blinking. –This is what you wanted right? –How did you know? –I know. –But how did you know? She looked down, -It's in your eyes. –In my eyes? He didn't know what to say, so he said -I want to keep looking at you, putting the words as literal as possible. She nodded, eyes liquid, emotive as she squinted up at him. He approached and she sat, on his bed.

-Is it true that you shave your entire body, he blurted, his leg inches from hers. -It is not true, completely, she said, looking down, one of her purple nails picking at the cuticle of the other. –My taxi is waiting, she said, -I'll walk you to the exit. -It's easier if I go alone.

And the awkwardness of such a discussion, apparently left unlocked the door, on noon of the following day to send a -meet me, and her response: a hand shaking emoticon.

Arriving at separate times, she slipping off the boulevard through a back gate, and knowing or not knowing the maid, but speaking to her as if in control, whether it was a class issue or not; he wasn't sure.

He imagined it as a scene from 1001 Nights, even though it was afternoon in a guarded compound, in a wrecked city, and he had never gotten through Burton's florid introduction, and now sitting in his swivel chair, and holding himself to not get up, or reach, as she unveiled, possibly, as there are no cameras inside rooms, nor in hallways, despite rumors.

And so things, rapidly reaching a boiling point inside him, if not for her control and sitting on his bed and crying with her breasts between her arms, her skirt hiked like shorts, and he going to her, but not too close, for she held up her hand. –I'm damaged. –You're beautiful, not damaged, he said. –Don't touch me! You already have seen enough that you'll never marry me.

And then it was her open face, open hair and body, turning rose colored from the illumination of light through the upper crack in the window, and still her statement in the air, a question of his control or lack thereof, to have pushed boundaries even using her tears, by which there may have been a consummation, which led one to question what happened with the senior advisor in the north.

And after there was a cooling, almost extinguishing of those fires, and he a reckoning what exactly he was doing with a foreign girl, over a decade younger than he, who he didn't really know, or how to speak to, and he wasn't sure of emotionally, but whom he had to work with.

A Bad Evening

Until came the evening when the older brother discovered her phone open in their tiled kitchen and looked at her screen, and recognized words on the screen in that language and took the phone to his friend who had been an interpreter for the occupier's army, and the friend told him the general tone of the messages, implying without saying so, that not only did his younger sister appear to have a boyfriend, but the boyfriend was most likely of the occupier origin. FoleyBook_Whereupon, that evening the girl's rice and lamb dish was cast on the floor as a gesture of what she'd done to their honor, and she repaired to her room, of concrete walls with no windows decorated with stuffed animals, a stereo system, a pink soccer scarf nailed to the wall, as seen in the photo shown to the reporter, and sat on the edge of her bed, blinked at the cracked marble floor and realized they'd taken her phone.

Where upon the girl returned to the living room and admitted that she didn't work at the Ministry of Trade, that she in fact worked for a partner government agency, and had for the past year, and the oldest brother, thinking of the time he'd seen the occupiers looking at her teenage body as prophecy, clenched and unclenched his right hand as he was want to do when completely baffled and wanted to hit something, and the younger shook his head. And the older said something to the effect of, you let them touch you to keep your job. You have no respect for yourself or your family!

-Touch me? she screamed, -They're all old men, and nice to me, which didn't help, as the older brother, made her look him in the eye and to vow to quit as of immediately, and the girl reminded them she brought home the same money both of them did combined, where upon the older brother hurled her cell phone against the opposite wall, and said if she tried to go back to the compound they'd lock her in the house.

Whereupon the girl began to cry as she managed to separate her SIM card from the wreckage of her phone.

Communication Black Out

No text or call came to the compound from her destroyed phone, nor was she able to answer the multiple calls placed by the reporter or the communications director.

She didn't show up for work for three days, and the communication's director hobbled to the HR department to ensure she was fired, further proving to the reporter, the jealousy of the older woman towards the local, who, despite being of the tattered country, still had hopes and dreams.

He sent her multiple emails of concern, warning: a miasma of guilt settling in, to no avail, and as happens when there is nothing a compound expatriate can do, asked another girl to check at her house. Whereupon the other girl returned, and said the older brother had told her, she'd been sent to relatives out of the country.

Such was the drop in his stomach, indicating that he cared more than he thought, even he thought it was a lie, as logic stated she would have immigrated at first chance. And exactly an hour later came the text-

Hi! Im in my house, my bros, won't let me leave. They made me quit after they found our texts. They say Im dirty, that no one will want me, not even a foreigner cause Im a liar, cuz there Is No Future Here. Tell the boss I can't come in anymore. I don't know how I can see you again.He registered the reaching tone, the dozens of phrases to reply as he lay down that night, and not coming up with any, of how to save her honor, he felt himself sinking into the casing of an invertebrate with no limbs or brain, only clouded feelings.

The reporter might have done better to analyze the psychological effect of a previous year's worth of yearning for simple and suitable female companionship and for action as opposed to desk sitting, added by a fixation on seeing her hair free again, and certain other images of her, all conditioned by the compound, in that none of these feelings were real, in an objective sense, but being situated in the compound, it proved difficult to evaluate. It would have helped to go outside for a minute.

Hunting Club
His only glimpse of freedom in the city had consisted of the night he'd snuck off the compound, to the Hunting Club in the once posh neighborhood, on the other side of the uncompleted mosque, to meet the assistant who used to be a manager for the country's first cell phone company, located just outside the compound, and now the assistant to the chief of party.

And of seeing a hall of young shisha smokers surrounded by eighties stand up video game consuls, a banquet hall serving western beers and whiskies with lamb and rice dishes, shrubbery lit by colored lights as if to shine through perceptions on the guarded compound on the opposite side of the mosque.

He imbibed as if he was a man with no county or compound to return to, and things got so blurry he stumbled towards a group of men smoking with serious faces, who called him a bad word, loosely translated as fuck head, and his friend, the assistant to the chief of party, had to make an excuse for him, that he was from another country, not the colonizer one, but the one bordering it to the north.

A Kind of Plan

And having established mutual confidences, the reporter brought to the assistant, in one of the compound's furthest gardens, heavy with generator gargle, the issue of wanting to make a change for the girl, as in confidentially asking him to go to her house, to arrange a meeting for them at the same hunting club.

The assistant lit a foreign cigarette, and said it was impossible to arrange a meeting with an unmarried woman without inviting her family, and the reporter asked what this meant, and the assistant said to meet with her, he had to bring her brothers, and they would most likely insist he engage her. -Meaning what exactly? -You know what it means, the assistant replied.

To which the reporter asked if this was mandatory, to which the assistant laughed and then said in a serious manner, it was a matter of respect, as even he wouldn't allow the reporter such a meeting with his own sister unless it was done in this manner. To which the reporter said, -Let me be honest. I'm thinking of marrying her, to which the assistant said, -Bro, you don't even know her family. —So, he replied? -So how can you know what kind of girl she is?

-I'm thinking I'm going to marry her so she can get her papers, he modified. —But are you sure you want to do that? the assistant asked.

And the reporter swore it wasn't his need for companionship or belief she was the one, that he felt responsible for her brothers finding out, and that he knew it was all about the passport, or green card, or however a foreign spouse got access to one's citizenship following the prescribed wait time.

Privately, he said, he didn't want anything from her, and was far from being tagged a sex pat, as they referred to the graying men who spent their tax-free remuneration on far eastern trips to find young pieces of things to suction themselves on to, or those kind of women who, perhaps for reasons of being seen as overweight in their country, returned with strapping, usually darker men on their arms.

Even with these certainties, the reporter did not sleep well, the night he was supposed to sleep on it, and in the morning, woke, and before his first Nescafe, texted- I'll marry you so you can get a Visa, however long it takes, and pressed send.

Feeling the thrill of the decisive charge, as if impressed by drawing his own sword against a line of guns, he then settled into a troubled worrying, as if he'd fallen on it, followed by depression after lunch, queasily he went back to the assistant and told him he was ready. To which the assistant put his hand on the reporter's shoulder as if to steady him, and said- Are you sure you want to take her to your home?

To which the reporter felt even more vaguely uncertain and looked the assistant in the eyes and nodded solemnly. –Ok, it's ready the assistant said. And using the previous method, the reporter, snuck over the wall in the back yard of the business center, where there was a gap between the top of the wall and the covered chain link, a blind spot to the roof guards, and slipped under the fence and jumped down from the wall and entered a weedy garden in the dark, and shining his pocket light, walked the path to the dirt roundabout where the assistant was waiting for him in his Toyota.

The Meeting

And so at the hunting club he met the older brother, a heavy five o'clock shadow dressed in jeans and an orange woven turtleneck, and they sat on some cracked and peeling plastic couches, the assistant getting each a glass of whiskey from the bar.

The older brother with a jutting chin, possibly emboldened on meeting an office type, rather than the tattooed type who carried a gun, said -What makes you think I would allow my sister to marry an infidel occupier? To which the assistant translated the question as, -How much are you willing to show your sacrifice for the opportunity of the hand of my sister in marriage?

To which the reporter said, -Whatever I can offer to show my sincerity, within what I can afford and still provide for my family, the truth being he had professional level parents with good retirements going. To which the assistant replied to the brother, -I will make whatever sacrifices to you to prove that I am worthy.

To which the brother replied, -It is not a matter of money, you lying dog, unless you become a believer you will not marry her. To which, the assistant replied, -It is not a matter of money and you have to go through a religious ceremony.

To which the reporter answered, -I will make sure she has a good life always, which stabbed of hyperbole, and told a story of seeing a foreign solider who knelt to pray with a mother who's son's leg had been blown off playing soccer in the street.

The reporter didn't actually witness this sequence, but told it as a prelude to saying two peoples whose fates were entangled could pray together in the worst times, even if of opposite faiths, which the reporter felt right about saying, and which the assistant embellished somewhat for understanding.

Whereby the brother paused, took a sip of his whisky and not seeming to swallow, said he would be better able to consider the sincerity of the subject by the dowry, as per the country's marriage contracts, to which the assistant got tired and said, -He wants money, it's part of the law, but he thinks you are rich.

To which the reporter replied, tell him a Visa to my country includes family members after five years, which the assistant didn't, but said he could offer double the going rate of 350 in the occupier's currency.

-Triple, the brother said, and rose, downing the rest of his whiskey in one gulp, -This will not affect me he mumbled and walked away.

So, it was an issue of momentum, he'd already begun with this proud, if crude man, and the reporter knew that he couldn't back down, and through the force of his own will, he was to forge the path to an arrangement that would help her immensely.

He withdrew, rather, cash advanced on his next pay check, triple the going rate of a groom dowry and handed the money over to the assistant, who said -Are you sure, to which the reporter said -Yes, which naturally set in motion the contract.

Last Trip North

Communications proposal: to go report on an energy advisor's intervention in the assembling of drilling simulators for a refinery whose engineers had never been trained to assemble them, a story said advisor had been nagging him to do. The director, lightly puffing Ultra Lights, her eyes beatific from freshly mailed pills, had re-submitted her resignation, and management had taken her up on it, and she was now subtly fighting efforts to be flown out of country, by showing initiative, and agreed to send a signed request for the reporter's plane ticket.

To the deputy chief of party, facilitated by personal delivery, the reporter hovering in his office, while the deputy, a man of unusual mass, signed on the line.

And packing one suit, rather suit jacket, a borrowed tie, his maid-pressed white shirt and the blessing of the assistant, as to the swirly mess in his mind, he reconciled himself to start the paperwork, meaning the religious conversion, the blood test, and the payment of the officiate, whose offices had multiplied as license requests increased in proportion to the decrease in random bloodletting.

Although five separate suicides set off concussions across the city, throwing dozens of bodies in the face of officials set to run for national re-election based on security improvements, the reporter was lost in his own problems that began with her journey northward. Death was not on his radar screen.

And so he flew to the northern province, where he texted the girl he would meet her, having provided for her trip, with brothers, in a five hour taxi ride, arranged through the assistant, to the hotel, where he would not officially stay, as being a non-speaker, still required one armed chaperone, and a stay in the province's compound.

But having communicated electronically with the actual energy advisor, admitting his trip a ruse with a rendezvous attached, to which the advisor, a big-bellied man from a rural area, replied in typically over-accented, the reporter believed, lexicon, -You fornicating son of a gun, indicating admiration, and that he would indeed sign him on the safety list when the reporter slipped away for the night, using a hired taxi, purportedly to enjoy both his marriage duties and rights.

The White Hijab

A ceremony in a small sized conference room, with a man in a shiny suit, two passport sized photos, his hand on the holiest of their books, and words to the effect that there was only one prophet of the book he had his hand on, and the light touch of her hand over his hand, over the book.

The formality of which, most singularly centered on the snowy whiteness of her hijab, attached to a bodice of satin and sequins and a rather flat, long dress, eyes heavy bluish and lips reddened; he in a tweed suit coat and tie forgotten. As they touched the gilded cover, a half whisper caught in her voice, -You saved my life. And he -It's not over yet.

Brothers, one standing stonily, the other with hands folded, to the side, and a waiter, as a witness, texting, probably his own love, and the silence after the judge ended speaking his pronouncements or blessings. The reporter not sure to address her directly, or her brothers through her interpretation, as in a statement of appreciation, or stand to the side with respectful posture, chose to remain quiet.

Her own face bright, but aware of being watched by both brothers and reporter, and the impossibility of pleasing any of them, before all repairing to the recommended restaurant, adjacent, where the tasting of carp flesh slow burned in wood charcoal lessened the need to talk.

The older brother modeling how to gouge out the flesh with ones fingers, nodding when the reporter managed a good piece into his mouth.

Then, the brothers were smoking outside, and he turned with the question that had been waiting. –When do we leave them? Her face, a pleased daze, turned. -But I can't go with you. -What do you mean? She winced -You know what this was for. And he reached for her lap –Ok, give me that paper. -You want to do that? –Give it to me! his whisper a static hiss.

She reached in her purse, also white. But he held her hand there, realizing he wouldn't take it and that he wanted to take it and tear it, and her white hijab, her make-up, everything and to find what she was really about, and then punch her oldest brother, to make him bleed. Instead, he paid their restaurant bill.

The younger brother taking her for the elevator. The older brother clenching and unclenching his hands. No one said anything. The older brother nodded, –Are you sure I can get a Visa too?

It might have been better if the brother had laid the reporter unconscious on the lobby marble, his mind sifting through his ear like fine sand; instead, he found himself alone at the restaurant bar on the top floor, the same place where the senior advisor had taken her.

Black Label whisky, and mushy mouthed to the recently arrived Filipina in the burgundy vest, until he bummed a cigarette and puked up all the carp in a urinal. Got the spins and a sudden rush of heat, and laid down on the tile under the urinal with his copy of the receipt for his blood work, check results in two weeks.

The manager, deferential to westerners, nudged him awake with his foot, and the reporter thought he saw a hook nosed devil just before he got up and apologized.

Text message the next morning, as he found himself somehow in the room he'd intended to share with her, his shoes still on, no blood work receipt, I'm very happy! Thank you for everything!

He wanted to reply - go Fuck yourself! but decided he already had fucked his karma. So paying the hotel bill in cash, returning in a taxi to the airport, flying back to the capital after a two-hour delay, a certain ripped feeling in his stomach, and the security team waiting for him, one of the mercenary giants smiled –Did you have a good time sir? -Sure.

Riding back in the armored convoy, he couldn't have predicted the color of the deeply burnt sun set over the tan boxed buildings, the street full of mini-buses of girls coming from the girls' school, two boys on a scooter, one facing backwards one forwards, two salesmen arguing in front of their rows of pointy-toed shoes, a bombed out ice cream parlor.

The communications director who although ill through the latter half of her tenure, was prescient enough to read the unclosed chats, left open on the girl's computer, and seeing discussions regarding her illness, and herself termed CRAZY, in capital letters by the reporter, with googly emoticons added by the girl, decided, before she was flown out of the country, the security detail instructed to watch her getting on the actual plane, to put her brand of hex on the two.

And so the next morning, the assistant, the only one the reporter could trust, called in the reporter and told him a meeting had been requested of him with the deputy and the chief regarding his trip.

And he didn't understand how he could already begin to sweat, how his hands tremored, how the body betrays all, as he texted her, as he walked towards the deputy's office. -I think they know. She texted back, -Know what?

Tangled Web of Half-Truths
The second problem being the country-accented advisor, who had covered for him the night of the wedding, had a relationship with the aforementioned senior advisor, based on the latter's relationship to the prime minister's advisory council, and the former to consulting on new oil fields now priming, and using those quid pro quos as a currency:

The county-accented advisor offered the information of said reporter traveling to the northern province for a rendezvous, revealing reporter's critical mistake in distribution of information, whereupon the senior advisor realized, based on information left in an email by the director of communications, the reporter was most likely rendezvousing with the girl, the one who hadn't even let him touch her in secret, not even with her clothes on, after all he had done for her, and so sent an email to the deputy chief.

When all information was brought to the deputy, the reporter was accused of misuse of gov't. funds, having falsified the rational for his trip and also violating contractually security terms.

All laid in front of him, in the form of photocopied plane ticket stubs and armored escort spread sheets, and he, as all expats, had an at will contract, meaning dismissal, wheneverfor whatever, which rarely happened as the company made money by fielding boots, or wingtips, in the case of senior advisors, on the ground, tipping the top range of gov't pay scales. And, not being close to the top tier or having any favors due with high-ranking host country officials, did not help the reporter.

The brimstone in the deputy's face, and a twinge of empathy in the chief's. The instinct he could blink it away, and when he blinked, saw the desk, photocopies of his travel documents, the bulk of the deputy and sad sack posture of the chief. Policy was policy, condolences were exchanged. The apology one sided.

Advisors all had their plans- the next contract, bigger bump, higher profile, their schemes mental life rafts, always about to come due, and so the reporter didn't advise anyone of his termination, as the compound's hunger for misfortunes, its lusting suck hole, was in the details that would be revealed at the appointed time, with him gone, and leaving a last bone wasn't in him. There was barely the energy to pack, his camera, boots, a bag full of dress shirts to give the assistant.

What's Left?
And so from inside the guarded enclave, came a three-car convoy of four-door Suburbans, the reporter in the middle car, with two bags packed in the trunk, the last weave through the T-Walls, a glimpse of the local guard in the tattered police uniform presiding over the ruins of a place so incomprehensible, its founder named it the city of peace.

And so the older brother would be stopped at a checkpoint, weeks later, where they would break his arm for working with the occupiers, ironically, and put a barrel loaded with a bullet to his head, and pause as the occupiers were rolling by in their armored omnibus and the man in the turret would look down on the bleeding brother and do nothing, but coincidentally save him.

Later, the younger would be drinking alcohol in another suburb, and men in masks would stop him and put a gun in his window and he would grab the barrel from the driver's seat, shouting —do you know who I am? And, they would say to stop, and he didn't let go, repeating, I'm Zaid, so a gun punctured his head from the other window. And the girl would not know this, for days.

-Can you drop me on the other side, the reporter asked the driver with oaken forearms, -It's the military air side, sir. -That's what I'm taking, sir.

The driver smiled, -More adventures sir, the reporter said nothing. Thinking of how he would email the girl from a base in the North after she'd already heard of his departure. How he would sound more confident to her. How she would hear it in his voice.

And the girl named Mirage would hold still, barely leaving or going from the enclosure of her house now filling with ghosts, until the assistant to the advisor got a call from anofficiate asking about confirmation to a marriage license, as the reporter had for reason of language barrier, left the assistant's number as his own, and the assistant informed Mirage and she would feel lifted, as to the promise of, as to leaving, as soon as she got the money. The reporter promised he would be sending her some as soon as he got it.

Contributors

Benjamin Balthaser is assistant professor of U.S. multi-ethnic literature at Indiana University, South Bend. His collection of poems on the lives of blacklisted Jewish activists, Dedication, appeared from Partisan Press in 2011. His forthcoming book from the University of Michigan Press, Anti-Imperialist Modernism, excavates the role of anti-imperialist movements in the construction of radical modernist culture. Other critical and creative work of his has appeared or is forthcoming in The Minnesota Review, The Massachusetts Review, American Quarterly, The Oxford History of the Novel, and elsewhere. He lives in Chicago, and bicycles by the Pilsen mural to Jim weekly, where it continues to both move and haunt him.

Matt Basiliere has an MFA in fiction from the University of Massachusetts, Amherst. He lives and works outside of Boston and has fiction forthcoming in Verdad.

C.S. Carrier is the author of Mantle (H_NGM_N Books 2013). He lives in Clarksville, AR. He thinks of Jim Foley often.

Yago S. Cura is an Adult Services Librarian at the Vernon branch of the Los Angeles Public Library in sunny South Central Los Angeles. He is a former N.Y.C. Teaching Fellow and A.L.A. Spectrum Scholar who also happens to publish the poetry, fiction, and prose of authors from las Américas in Hinchas de Poesía (www.hinchasdepoesia.com) with Jim Heavily and Jennifer Therieau. Yago has self-published Rubberroom (HINCHAS, 2010), and in 2010, he co-wrote Odas a Futbolistas (HINCHAS, 2012) with Abel Folgar, and has completed Postcard Feats (HINCHAS, 2011) with C.S. Carrier and Jim Heavily. Yago's poetry has appeared in Huizache, KWELI, PALABRA, Borderlands, Lungfull!, COMBO, LIT, U.S. Latino Review, 2nd Avenue, Exquisite Corpse, FIELD, and Slope. His reviews have appeared in The St. Mark's Poetry Project Newsletter. Along with Ryan Nance, he is the co-founder of the Copa Poetica (http://copapoetica.us), a three day reading series in Los Angeles on the rest days of the 2014 World Cup. His Spanglish blog, Spicaresque (http://spicaresque.blogspot.com), has had more than 55,000 visitors. From 2013 to 2015, 61% of the 18-24 year olds sitting in Yago's English classes inside the Los Angeles County Jail were able to pass the E.L.A./C.A.H.S.E.E.

Mike Dockins was born in 1972 and grew up in Yonkers NY. He holds a B.S. from SUNY Brockport (1999), an MFA from UMASS Amherst (2002), and a PhD from Georgia State University (2010). His poems have appeared in Crazyhorse, The Gettysburg Review, Third Coast, The Greensboro Review, Quarterly West, Willow Springs, Salt Hill, Atlanta Review, jubilat, Mid-American Review, Bateau, Indiana

Review, Gulf Coast, West Branch, Meridian, PANK, and elsewhere, and they have been reprinted on Poetry Daily, Verse Daily, and in the 2007 edition of The Best American Poetry. His critically-acclaimed first book of poems, Slouching in the Path of a Comet (Sage Hill Press, 2007), after moving 850 copies, is currently anticipating re-issue. His second collection, Letter to So-and-So from Wherever, won the Maxine Kumin Award in Poetry,and was published by C&R Press in November 2014. For the last 15 years he has taught creative writing with John Hopkins University's Center for Talented Youth (CTY) summer program. Mike moonlights as a singer-songwriter. Fame For Zoe, a full-length album (2005) from his acoustic-pop duo Clop, is available on iTunes. Mike uses his various credentials to enjoy periodic unemployment, periodic homelessness, and chronic jadedness toward Academia.

Rachelle Escamilla is the host of #OutofOurMInds the 2nd-longest running #PoetryRadio show in the country. She is also the Author of Imaginary Animal (Willow Books, 2015), the founder of the Poets & Writers Coalition at S.J.S.U., and the co-founder of Mainland China's first creative writing center (at SYSU in Guangzhou). Hit her up at the web address, www.poetita.com.

Martín Espada Martín Espada has published more than fifteen books as a poet, editor, essayist and translator. His forthcoming collection of poems is called Vivas to Those Who Have Failed (2016). Other books of poems include The Trouble Ball (2011) The Republic of Poetry (2006), and Alabanza (2003). His honors include the Shelley Memorial Award, the PEN/Revson Fellowship and a Guggenheim Fellowship. The Republic of Poetry was a finalist for the Pulitzer Prize. The title poem of his collection Alabanza, about 9/11, has been widely anthologized and performed. His book of essays, Zapata's Disciple (1998), has been banned in Tucson as part of the Mexican-American Studies Program outlawed by the state of Arizona. A former tenant lawyer, Espada is a professor of English at the University of Massachusetts-Amherst.

Clare Morgana Gillis is a historian and journalist. She completed a PhD in medieval history in 2010 and has worked in the Middle East as a journalist since then. She is spending the academic year 2015-16 teaching college in New England.

Kevin Goodan is an American poet and professor. His most recent book is Winter Tenor. His first book, In the Ghost-House Acquainted, won a New England/New York Award from Alice James Books, as well as the 2005 L.L. Winship/PEN New England Award.

Adolfo Guzman-Lopez is a poet and journalist. In 1994 he co-founded the performance-poetry group The Taco Shop Poets, which toured nationwide, published, and recorded two CDs. His writing explores the changing Southern California neighborhoods, love, how to talk to children, and the cyclical/clockwork elements of spirituality. He's been a reporter at NPR-affiliate KPCC 89.3FM in Los Angeles since 2000. He's been awarded the LA Press Club's "Radio Journalist of the Year" and other journalism honors. He was born in Mexico City, grew up in Tijuana and San Diego, and currently lives in Long Beach, CA.

Daniel Johnson befriended James Foley while they were Teach for America corps in Phoenix, Arizona from1996 to 1999. During that time, they made a pact together to become writers and took early writing workshops with the Writer's Voice at the Phoenix YMCA. Over nearly two decades of friendship, they often traveled together including tripsto Mexico, Cuba, and New York City in 2008 to protest George W. Bush's second inauguration. Daniel is the author of How to Catch a Falling Knife published by Alice James Books in 2010. His writing has been featured on PBS News Hour, NPR, and in publications such as The Washington Post, Boston Globe, and The Best American Poetry 2007. Johnson is the founding executive director of 826 Boston, a youth writing center, which is part of the national network founded by writer Dave Eggers. Johnson lives with his wife and children in Boston. A prize possession of his remains his copy of The Unabridged Letters of Sylvia Plath, a gift from James Foley. Scrawled across the title page, it reads, "DJ- Fuck it believe – Jimmy '06."

Brian Jordan received his MFA from the University of Massachusetts at Amherst. He writes fiction and teaches in Boston.

Daniel Mahoney is a writer and translator whose work has appeared in many journals. He is the author of Sunblind Almost Motorcrash, a book and cassette project out from Spork Press in 2015. He teaches literature and writing at College of the Atlantic in Bar Harbor, Maine.

Susie Meserve is a poet, essayist, and memoirist whose work has appeared in The New York Times, Salon, and Elle, as well as in many literary journals. She is also the author of a chapbook of poems, Faith. She is on the faculty of Academy of Art University and lives in Berkeley, California, with her husband and young son.

D.N. Pace is a teacher and an author from Columbus, Indiana. She wishes to thank all those involved in the Ghazals for Foley project. She feels especially honored to be a part of it.

Ethan Paquin's most recent book of poems is Cloud vs. Cloud (Ahsahta Press, 2013). New poems are forthcoming in The Laurel Review and Conduit, among other journals. He attended the MFA Program for Poets & Writers at the University of Massachusetts with Jim.

Yaddyra Peralta is a poet who teaches writing and literature at Broward College and Miami Dade College. She has work forthcoming in Eight Miami Poets (Jai Alai

Books). Her poems have also appeared in Ploughshares, Jai Alai, Abe's Penny, Tigertail, The New Poet, and Hinchas de Poesia. In 2013, she was a Visiting Writer at the Betsy Hotel's Writer's Room in South Miami Beach, Florida and one of six collaborative Helen M. Salzberg Artists-in-Residence at Florida Atlantic University's Jaffe Center for the Book Arts where she contributed to the collaborative artists' book Conversation, Too (Extra Virgin Press). She is poetry editor at Sliver of Stone and Assistant Director at the Palm Beach Poetry Festival.

Connolly Ryan was born in Greenwich Village, New York in 1967. He received both a BA in English and an MFA in Poetry from UMass, Amherst. Between degrees he traveled in Ireland and Oregon. A quote by G.K. Chesterton which applies to Connolly's own life and philosophy: "An adventure is only an inconvenience rightly considered. An inconvenienceis an adventure wrongly considered." He is currently a resident of Florence, Mass. and a professor of literature here at University of Massachusetts where he was thrice a finalist for the Distinguished Teaching Award. His visceral and witty poetry has been published in various journals including Scythe, Silkworm, Harvard Review, Slope, Meat For Tea, Pannax Index, and Old Crow. He is also a multiple Pushcart nominee. He has two finished Manuscripts: Fort Polio, and The Uncle Becky Chronicles. He is excited and inspired to be exploring the art of writing to such a dynamic gaggle of diverse perspectives.

Shauna Seliy met Jim at an orientation for UMass graduate T.A.s assigned to teach freshman composition. That was in the fall of 1999. They are still friends all these many years later, despite the time, distance, and seemingly permanent separation.

Sejal Shah's writing has been nominated for Best American Essays and the Pushcart Prize, and featured in The Huffington Post. Her essays and stories appear in Brevity, Conjunctions (Web), The Kenyon Review, The Literary Review, The Margins, The Massachusetts Review, and others. She lives and teaches in Rochester, NY; her website address is www.sejal-shah.com.

Chris Van Dyke used to write a lot of poems, but currently spends most of his time raising his three children and six chickens in Bed-Stuy, Brooklyn. He teaches his high school students to never discuss a poem until they've read it at least three times, and thinks this is generally the best life advice he has to offer anyone.

Andrew Varnon is a freelance writer and lecturer in English and Journalism at Western New England University. He lives in Greenfield with his wife and their two children and scruffy dog.

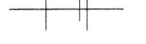

www.HINCHASPress.com

www.ingramcontent.com/pod-product-compliance
Lightning Source LLC
Chambersburg PA
CBHW072105290426
44110CB00014B/1837